FOUR IN NUMEROL OGY

MARCIA BATISTE WILSON

CW00498372

FOUR IN NUMERLOGY

To find out

what number

is for your

name, look at

the chart and

place the

number

under each

letter of your

full name.

Add all the

numbers

together. If

you get a

double digit,

add the two

numbers

together. If

you get

another

double digit

add the

numbers

together and

that will be

your name

number. Here

is the chart:

1 is a-j-s

2 is b-k-t

3 is c-l-u

4 is d-m-v

5 is e-n-w

6 is f-o-x

7 is g-p-y

8 is h-q-z

9 is i-r

4 in

numerology

in human

relationships

desires to be

popular, to

be loved, and

to love as a

basic part of

the nature.

They have

many

interesting

experience

and the

happenings

are so many,

odd, and

emotional

that a story

book or

novel could

be written

about its life.

Three has

many talents.

It turns raw

material into

particular

forms,

shapes, and

molds them

into harmony

with each

other. This

number has

high

standards for

honesty,

courage, the

gifts of

concentration

, application,

the ability to

appraise and

evaluate

worth and

value. Bless

GOD.

References

Jordan, Juno. Numerology: The Romance in Your Name. Devorss Company.

Marina Del Rey, California.

Printed in Great Britain
by Amazon

28462333R00020